Sumary of COMMAND

Alice Evans

Table of contents of

Chapter 1

Chapter 2

Chapter 1

One of our most distinguished military historians is Lawrence Freedman. He examines the marriage of powers that has occurred in the conduct of wars after 1945 in his scholarly new book Command, based on decades of research. He examines where political authority meets military skill and who ultimately has the last word.

This connection, inevitably, differs significantly between totalitarian nations and western democracies. For example, Khrushchev during the Cuban Missile Crisis, Saddam Hussein during the two Gulf Wars, or (and this book is very up to current) Putin's invasion of Ukraine are examples of the latter, when the military leadership and political authority are one and the same. According to Freedman, these leaders are guys (and they are always all males) who are surrounded by adoring generals who have discovered that the only way to survive is to concur with whatever the leader wants to do.

Unsurprisingly, this is the reason why so many tyrants fail. Khrushchev was overthrown shortly after the Cuban Missile Crisis because he disregarded the few people who cautioned him that the Americans would forcibly prevent Russia from putting Cuba's nuclear armament at their doorstep. General Galtieri, the ruler of Argentina, didn't seem to be aware that the United Kingdom would send a task force 8,000 miles away to free the Falkland Islands twenty years later. And many of us still remember the shocked amazement on the faces of two ursine Russian generals at one of Putin's news briefings when he declared that he was upping the nuclear stakes—obviously without consulting his military leaders—after his assault on Ukraine began to go poorly.

Because of this, it is more fascinating when Freedman looks at instances in democracies when the military forgets who is in power.

knowledgeable, perceptive, and masterful One has a suspicion that every Nato officer aspiring to high command will soon be forced to read this well-researched, well-written, and thought-provoking book. One of our most distinguished military historians is Lawrence Freedman.

He examines the marriage of powers that has occurred in the conduct of wars after 1945 in this insightful work, based on decades of research: where political authority meets military skill, and who ultimately has the last word. . Sumptuous... this should be the required reading for military history courses in staff colleges all across the globe.

In this broad survey of command in war since 1945, Lawrence Freedman brings to bear his extensive knowledge to explain the many complexities commanders at the highest level must now face, from grasping new ways of warfare to managing military organization and supply and, above all, coping with the mercurial behavior of their political masters. If there is a theme to Freedman's book, which runs from the Korean War to Putin's 'special military operation' in Ukraine, it is to be found in the tensions and disputes between military officers and the politicians who call the shots that he describes.

How often must a great leader have wished he were free to do what he wanted? Politics often has to be taken into account. How difficult it has gotten to handle conflict is one of the discoveries of Freedman's thorough and knowledgeable work. .. [an] useful overview of the difficulties of contemporary command

Since 1950, Freedman has provided good, succinct descriptions of some of the major conflicts worldwide. When the author wraps up this helpful work, he makes an uplifting point:

"The benefits of democratic systems do not rest in their power to stop terrible choices from being made by leaders or governments. Their capacity to recognize these errors, learn from them, and adjust gives them an edge. Closed systems that forbid subordinates from raising uncomfortable issues will suffer from this." Command, in which he distills a lifetime of research into the nature and practice of war, is undoubtedly his best work. It is fluidly written and persuasively argued.

Richard Freedman
provides a comprehensive summary of the global history of current conflicts
presents several case studies, draws analogies, and significant conclusions concerning the use of command
combines the political and military history of leadership in the post-World War II period.

Making sure that commands are suitable, effectively delivered, and then followed is what command in a conflict is all about. But the process is also quite political.

This is mostly due to the fact that how conflicts are waged heavily relies on how their objectives are determined. Additionally, commanders in one domain must be able to cooperate with other command structures, including those of allies and different branches of the military.

 In Command, Lawrence Freedman uses a series of eleven vivid case studies, all from the time after 1945, to examine the significance of political as well as operational considerations in command. Civil conflicts replaced great power clashes during this time, and advancements in communication technology made it simpler for higher-level commanders to give orders to their subordinates.

Freedman discusses both wins and losses. In 1971, while Pakistan was losing the eastern portion of its territory to India, its generals made an effort to delay capitulation. Saddam Hussein of Iraq spun his setbacks into stories of triumph. In 2001, Osama bin Laden eluded American forces in Afghanistan. After 2003, the UK struggled in Iraq as a junior partner to the US.

 We encounter disobedient generals who twice attempted to overthrow their political authority, including Arik Sharon of Israel and those in the French army in Algeria. On the other extreme, Che Guevara in the Congo in 1966 and Igor Girkin in the Ukraine in 2014 both attempted to start small-scale battles in order to further their larger-than-life goals.

According to Freedman, authority—the capacity to issue orders—is the definition of command. nevertheless, give command's ability to make judgments top priority. In my opinion, commanders have the most power in this area. There seems to be little difference. According to me, since commanders are acknowledged as decision-makers, they have the authority to give instructions to their subordinates and choose when, where, and how to deploy them.

The official expression of command decisions is an order. According to Freedman, the power to issue orders is the most important one, albeit is usually followed by a choice. The two conceptions of command are thus clearly tied to one another. Additionally, we are both intrigued by how the institution of command fosters organizational coherence. The definition of a research challenge, however, may significantly modify a research program, as his review well illustrates. Detail is crucial in definitional disputes.

Chapter 2

Command was never an individual power for me; it was always a social activity because I was interested in how decisions were made. It was more likely to be found in the interactions and relationships between commanders, their staffs, deputies, and subordinates than in the person of the leader.

Based on the idea of decision-making, the headquarters' lifeworld—rather than specific commanders—became the crucial subject of my analyses almost by default. Using his alternative concept of command as a foundation, Freedman challenges two key ideas in my argument. My book's main thesis is that, compared to the twentieth century, command has evolved into a more professionalized, collaborative activity known as "collective command." Freedman is skeptical about collective leadership and thinks that commanders have always had the option of distributing power. Less has changed for Freedman than I would have you believe; collective leadership is nothing new to him. He makes a really important argument that deserves attention.

Command has always been a group effort. As they do now, divisional commanders throughout the 20th century depended on staff officers, assistants, and headquarters; some divisional commanders even trusted their subordinates to make judgments. However, it is essential to be really clear about where and how decision-making has been shared in order to comprehend my case for communal leadership.

 The three components of command are leadership, mission management, and mission definition. Collective command does not imply the advent of command by committee or even a simple democratization of decision-making in each function. It alludes to an adjustment to the geography of command. Divisional commanders have really taken on progressively more individual responsibility for mission formulation, as I have argued throughout the whole book.

 Today's divisional commanders have far more control over deciding what their soldiers will actually perform in a theater of operations than their predecessors had in the twentieth century. The political and even military guidance given to generals in recent decades has often fallen short, as Freedman has shown better than other experts. Divisional commanders are now nodes in a politico-military complex that must work with several partners and agents to achieve a mission, despite their formal designation as simply tactical commanders. In fact, command responsibility has expanded at this level. Major Generals have never been more crucial.

However, despite taking on more responsibility for mission description, divisional commanders are still required to delegate decision-making power when it comes to managing missions. Military operations now include a wide range of troops and varied participants, making coordination highly challenging.

An analysis of the real-world of military decision-making was attempted in Command. As Freedman correctly notes, the book was undoubtedly constructed in a certain manner as a result of the definition of command, which characterized it as decision-making rather than authority. This has undoubtedly resulted in omissions and prejudices. His comment on the two potentially distinct meanings of command, however, also draws attention to the historical premise that forms the basis of the book.

One might persuasively argue that, as Freedman indicates, authority was the primary way that command was defined in the 20th century; generals gave commands. They were able to do this because choices should be made by an individual since operations were lineal and Newtonian, carried out by uniform ground troops under their direct leadership. Generals, however, are often unable to exercise conventional forms of command in the age of complex, joint, hybrid, and heterogeneous operations; they can no longer just direct their subordinates to do certain actions.

But they are forced to make choices all the time. In addition to characterizing difficult circumstances, identifying potential courses of action, and gaining the support of superiors, colleagues, and partners via manipulation, negotiation, and persuasion, this sometimes requires giving direct commands.

According to Freedman's elegant definition, it could be plausible to claim that command has been replaced by decision-making in the twenty-first century. Divisions must coordinate the use of planes, helicopters, drones, long-range artillery, political engagement, and cyber, information, and psychological operations in addition to making more choices at the divisional level than in the past.

As a result, divisional commanders have given their subordinates, deputies, and designated staff officers the authority to make day-to-day management choices while reserving the most crucial ones for themselves. They haven't only let subordinates make choices on their own, though. They have actively worked to establish a command team so that choices are incorporated into the broader mission and coordinated with all divisional operations. This is where the comparison between James Mattis, Commander of the 1st Marine Division during the Iraq Invasion in March and April 2003, and Bernard Montgomery, General Officer Commanding 3rd Infantry Division during the Battle of France in May 1940, is illuminating. As divisional commanders, there are similarities between Montgomery and Mattis; they were both strong, charismatic generals.

Montgomery, however, consistently exerted directional control over his subordinates while keeping a close eye on their actions. Mattis undoubtedly kept the most crucial choices to himself and maintained regular contact with his subordinates.

The commander of the 3rd Marine Air Wing and he worked so closely together to command his formation, however, that they almost shared command of a true combined air-ground operation. In order to maintain perfect unanimity throughout the echelons, he aggressively empowered and taught his subordinates to make choices.

Mattis deliberately saw himself as the team's captain—a primus inter pares. Montgomery, in contrast, envisioned himself as a conductor, closely "grasping" activities while keeping his followers firmly under control. Therefore, Freedman fears that divisional leadership may have always had collaborative characteristics. He also questions if the adjustments I saw at the divisional level just reflect a compression of command rather than a fundamental reform of it.

Accordingly, Army and Army Group commanders of the 20th century exercised collective leadership; but, due to the large scope of their level of command, they were required to share power at that time, just as divisional commanders are required to do now.

Montgomery had to think about broader issues of the Alliance and joint operations, political and civic activity, and the press in his role as Army Group Commander in 1944–1945. Even as an Army Group Commander, however, his problems remained mostly military-related; the political issues mostly concerned internal Alliance politics (which he handled badly).

Additionally, he was exempt from close collaboration with the other services. Montgomery's strategy for D-Day was plainly a "combined" operation reliant on naval and aerial strength. Although tactical air power was sometimes significant, the Battle of Normandy and the European Campaign were not, for the most part, a really combined effort.

It was clear that top Allied aviation commanders disliked and found Montgomery difficult to deal with. Initially, the British Second Army and the American First Army, then starting in July 1944, the British Second Army and the Canadian First Army, were the ground forces Montgomery focused almost exclusively on as the commander of an Army Group. Montgomery went too far, but the point could still be made. Army generals in the 20th century oversaw ground troops and conducted military operations.

Since the Second World War, nuclear warfare, small-scale guerrilla land operations, and cyber interference have rebuilt and reinvented military leadership.

From the French Colonial Wars, the Cuban Missile Crisis, and the Bangladesh Liberation War to North

Vietnam's Easter Offensive of 1972, the Falklands War, the Iraq War, and Russia's wars in Chechnya and Ukraine, Freedman adopts a global perspective while methodically examining its practice and politics since 1945.

By underlining the political element of strategy, Freedman demonstrates how military choices cannot be made in isolation from civilian goals and how commanders now need to be adept at navigating both politics and conflict.

With a reflection on the future of command in a society that depends more and more on technology like artificial intelligence, Freedman closes the book. This is a comprehensive and insightful history of how command evolved in the postwar age and will be regarded as the last word on a key idea in both military and political affairs.

Printed in Great Britain
by Amazon

12900076R00020